HOAKES ISLAND
A FIENDISH PUZZLE ADVENTURE

Helen Friel and Ian Friel

LAURENCE KING PUBLISHING

LAURENCE KING

Laurence King Publishing
361–373 City Road
London EC1V 1LR
T + 44 (0)20 7841 6900
F + 44 (0)20 7841 6910
enquiries@laurenceking.com
www.laurenceking.com

A catalog record for this book is available
from the British Library.

ISBN: 978-1-78627-033-7

Printed in China, March 2018

Griffin Notebooks
Our Quality is Legendary!

YOU MADE IT!

Thank you, thank you, thank you, thank you for coming!
Hoakes Island is in great danger, and us too. We sent
Graark the seagull out to find the right person to help us.
That person is YOU!

I'm Rita—Rita Tamandua. What's the danger? I'll have to
explain as we go along—there's no time to lose.

Henry Hoakes, the owner of Hoakes Island amusement
park, went missing six years ago. We don't know what's
happened to him, but he left this notebook and this map
behind.

The notebook doesn't make much sense at the moment
because Henry left all the pages out of order, and I've
confused things a bit more by using the blank parts for my
memoirs. (Read them as we go. They're fascinating.)

Have you looked at the map yet? Henry left it to help us
on our journey.

You will need to **solve the puzzles** on each page of the
notebook, and then **use the map** to show you where to go
next. Find extra clues with the **special red lens**.

Did you remember to bring a pen or pencil with you?
It would be a good idea to **note down where we travel**
on the map. We can also use the boxes beside the map to
record anything useful we find along the way.

Ready? **Turn the page to start our adventure!**

This is me—Rita! I'm so pleased you could join us. My friends have run on ahead, but you may be able to spot a few of them using your red lens. I'll introduce you as soon as we've got time.

Remember those puzzles I mentioned? The first one is over on the right. I've managed to solve it—I am a genius, after all—but after this we're going to need your help.

I solved this puzzle by filling in the missing mathematical symbols in the blue circles.

They match these symbols on the northern point of the compass, which means we have to go north from the Start square on the map.

17 (+) 3   20

15 (−) 3   12

25 (÷) 5   5

If you look on the map, you'll see the square to the north of Start has the number 18 in it. So we need to **turn to page 18 to start our journey**.

Told you—I'm a genius, a real smarty-paws!

Out of Order

Wait, who's this "hard-hearted, double-dyed villain"? It sounds as though he knew Henry before he went missing. Maybe there's a clue in my memoirs ….

The tale of my early years is simple and sad. Kidnapped when little more than a pup, I was taken across the seas to join Gritty McFlitty's Grand Circus.

They trained me to do all sorts of tricks—balance a peanut on my nose, balance a tennis ball on my nose, balance a beach ball ... you get the picture. I even had to wear a clown costume. People in the circus audience used to call out things like "Oi, nosy, give us a turn!" or "Nozzle-features, stand on your nose!" It was too, too humiliating.

But then one day, a little boy came to the circus with his parents. Moved to tears by my plight, he begged them to buy my freedom. Sir Reginald and Lady Rowena Hoakes were kind people, and did what he asked. Gritty McFlitty drove a hard bargain, but they were the inventors of Hoakes' Patent Anti-Fart Powder and very rich.

Housewives!

Troubled by malodorous ODORS from Hubby?

Hoakes' Patent Anti-Fart Powder

A housewife writes: "Since using Anti-Fart Powder my house smells as fresh as a daisy!" Mrs E.B., Solihull

Their heartfelt appeals finally convinced Gritty McFlitty
to give me my freedom. Well, to be strictly accurate, it was
a case of heartfelt appeals and a very large pile of cash.

So began my days at their great house on Hoakes Island. And
my life with the little boy, who was, of course, Henry Hoakes.

That's enough for now! Let's go!

54
56   53
55

9 × 6 = 54

So here we are. Six years after Henry disappeared, and this scary letter arrived yesterday. **This is why we need your help!**

The Greenshore District Council
Greenshore House, Greenshore
Greenshire GRR1 GRR

The Occupiers
Hoakes Island
Off the Greenshore Coast
Greenshire

June 10, 1959

To Whom It May Concern

Compulsory Purchase of Hoakes Island

The council has been made aware that the property known as Hoakes Island is now without an owner. The last known owner, Mr. Henry Hoakes, disappeared six years ago and is legally presumed to be deceased.

This means that the council is within its rights to buy the island using a Compulsory Purchase Order. There is a pressing need for new executive apartments in the area, and PoodleCo International, a local developer, has come forward with a plan to pull down the old Hoakes Island amusement park and replace it with the aforesaid much-needed apartments. This is in line with the council's Policy No QG432 (a), "You Can Have Too Much Of A Good Thing."

It has come to our notice that you are a group of individuals living on the island and keeping the park rides in repair. Under the powers granted to the council under the "We Can Do Anything We Want" Act (1949) you are ordered to cease all maintenance work on Hoakes Island and to leave Hoakes Island within one week.

Our lawyers inform me that I am legally obliged to tell you that if you can prove that you are the owners of Hoakes Island, by producing the title deed, we will not be able to proceed with the Compulsory Purchase Order. In that unlikely event, you would be recognized as the lawful owners.

Yours faithfully,

Arnold Grotflick MB, BoB, DOO, B(e), DOO
Head of Public Niceness

Sunshine Towers

Come for a day, stay forever!

To begin with, we panicked. But then we came up with a plan, which I call "Plan Rita":

(a) Find a brave and clever human to help us - that's YOU, by the way;
(b) Find Henry's "What to Do in an Emergency" letter;
(c) Find the deed!

And now, let's get going. The next page we go to is … oh help. **Got any ideas?**

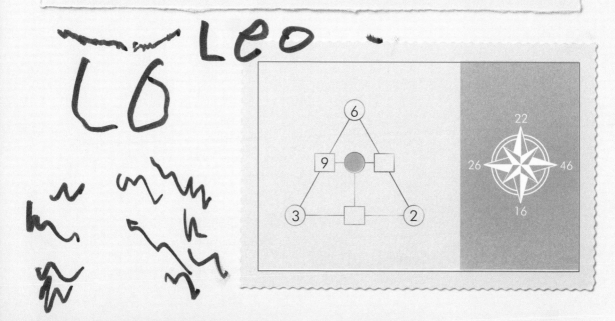

The first key! We must be on the right track. I don't know why it has a flag as a label, but Henry's put some flags and symbols on the map. **Note down the ones we find as we go along**—maybe they'll come in handy later.

As for the postcard that was in the envelope … hmm. **Can you see anything with the red lens?** If you spot something, remember to note it down!

THE GOLDILOCKS EXPERIENCE, HOAKES ISLAND

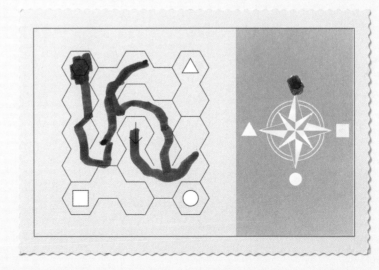

Hoakes House—at last! I'm in such a fluster I can't remember which door leads to the study—we'll have to use the house plan. It's on the map.

Each door to get inside the house has a number. If we can find the door that leads to the study I bet that number is also the number of the next page we need to turn to. I don't think we'll need the map any more! Maybe Henry is now giving us page numbers instead.

We were shocked when Henry disappeared. **Where could he have gone?** All he left was a note and this pile of papers on his desk. We knew that he had been planning his Grand Reveal, but even we didn't know what that actually was ....

May 21, 1953

My dear friends

    I'm sorry to leave you all like this, with no notice. I was hoping to give you the greatest surprise in history with my Grand Reveal—that's why I kept the surprise hidden until the last moment—only to discover that it had been stolen.

    Even now, I can't tell you what the surprise is, in case this note falls into the wrong hands. If it did, it would spark an international hunt that could bring disaster.

    The only clue I have suggests that the surprise was taken somewhere overseas. I will have to follow it, and if I can send you messages, I will. In order to keep my search secret, the messages may not be obvious ones.

    Don't worry about buying food or how to pay for the electricity, etc.—that's all taken care of. I've left instructions with the suppliers, and there is more than enough money to keep you all fed, watered, and warm for many, many years.

    I've left a "What to Do in an Emergency" letter. It will tell you what you need to do if anything goes wrong.

Love Henry

G&S

Gorblimey & Spode

ORDER FORM

Name..Henry Hoakes..............................

Address..Hoakes Island, Nr. Greenshore.

....

Quantity	Article
5	Ant pies (Rita)
200	Bananas (Granville)
3	Watermelons (Elvis + Dor..
14	Ice creams (Graark)
8	Bags of pumpkin seeds
11	Grass smoothies (Zoltan)
7	Sacks of carrots (Tina)
3	Bags of porridge oats
16	Sausages (Abel)

Griffin Notebooks
Our Quality is Legendary!

Dear Mr. Hoakes,

Thank you for your recent bespoke order. Red notebooks are currently out of stock so I have enclosed a blue one. I hope this meets your requirements.

Yours sincerely,

Hoaksie's lost his Grand Reveal,
How very sad he must feel

Want it back? Well, without fail
To the tropics you must sail!

You think it's in a case somewhere
Dead as a ..., with a glassy stare?

I'm really not all that hard-hearted
The ugly thing's back where it started!

DASH!
Morse Courses
Speedy Distance Learning

A	B	C	D
·—	—···	—·—·	—··
E	**F**	**G**	**H**
·	··—·	——·	····
I	**J**	**K**	**L**
··	·———	—·—	·—··
M	**N**	**O**	**P**
——	—·	———	·——·
Q	**R**	**S**	**T**
——·—	·—·	···	—
U	**V**	**W**	**X**
··—	···—	·——	—··—
	Y		**Z**
	—·——		——··

No....13.......

B&O Ferries
Making a Splash!

One-Way Ticket
One saloon cabin at the safer end of the ship

B&O Ferries

Rustbucket Line: Departures from Greenshore

Makeshift Line: Departures from Greenfleet

Bodge It Line: Departures from Greenhithe

Leak & Bail Line: Departures from Greeneggs

···· ·—· · ·
··— ·— —· —·— ·—··
·—·· ·— —· ·
·—— ·· — ···

Where do we go next?

15
16   14
13

A bit more Hoakes Island history ....

You may wonder why Hoakes Island is run by animals. Henry traveled a great deal, and spent a lot of time rescuing animals. Rather than just leave them to laze around, he gave them jobs. These are just a few of his great rescues:

The Hoakes Island zebras once belonged to Gritty McFlitty's Grand Cycling Stripey-Horse Troupe. Henry rescued them by getting the government to ban performing animals in circuses. (Mind you, for years afterward, you would find at least one Hoakes Island zebra riding in the Tour de France. One time, Zoltan even came close to winning the coveted Yellow Jersey.)

Henry found Granville working as a chef in a burger bar in downtown Bordeaux. It was a hot job, especially for someone covered in hair. Granville was delighted when Henry offered him a home. The customers of the burger bar were also delighted to get burgers with a little less hair in them.

SHAKE..........4
MILKSHAKE WITHOUT
  HAIR............5

SIDES
FRIES............2
MORE FRIES......4

KONG B
KONG MEG
KONG MEGA DO
KONG MEGA DOU
SUPER DUPER BU
KONG MEGA DOUBLE
SUPER DUPER EXTRA
BURGER.............

Burger Kong

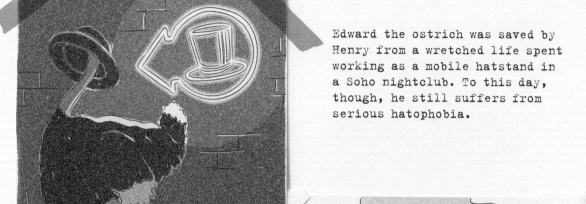

Edward the ostrich was saved by Henry from a wretched life spent working as a mobile hatstand in a Soho nightclub. To this day, though, he still suffers from serious hatophobia.

Elvis and Dorothy were also rescued by Henry. Well, not exactly rescued. They heard about him and then stowed away in his luggage when he returned from a trip to Uganda. They claim that they fled Africa because they belong to an endangered species. In my humble opinion what actually endangered them was the fact that they can be really, really, REALLY ANNOYING.

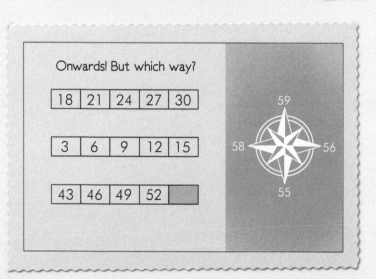

Onwards! But which way?

18	21	24	27	30

3	6	9	12	15

43	46	49	52	

59

58   56

55

Can you see the next envelope? Aha—at the top of those beanstalks.

But which one is safe to climb? I'm sure I saw something about beanstalks just now. **Go back a step and see if you can spot anything useful.** Once we've climbed the right beanstalk, perhaps we'll see which way to go next.

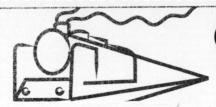

I've also used this notebook as a scrapbook.
It should help fill you in on what's happened.

Confused crowds at Hoakes Island

May 23, 1953
WORLD OF ENTERTAINMENT

HOAX AT HOAKES ISLAND?

By Sleazy McGleazy
Our Entertainment Correspondent

The world of entertainment was in shock last night. Henry Hoakes, creator of Hoakes Island amusement park, has vanished without trace. The future of his unique attraction is now extremely uncertain.

Heir to a fabulous family fortune, Hoakes has spent decades building his park. As is well known, all of the staff are dressed up as talking animals. In recent weeks, Hoakes has been hinting that "The Greatest Discovery in History" would be revealed on Hoakes Island this month. But now, one day after this "Discovery" was due to be revealed, Hoakes has disappeared, and the park is all locked up.

A local businessman, who did not want to be named, said this:

"Promises, promises. That's Henry Hoakes all over. I've known him for more years than I care to remember. I know what he's like. Hoakes's 'Grand Reveal' is no more than, er, a hoax. I bet he just ran off when he finally realized that the world would see him for what he is—a fraud!"

I tried to interview the staff at Hoakes Island, but most were too upset to reply. Bravely, they all kept their animal costumes on and a few tried to stay in character with a series of grunts, growls, squeaks, and ook-ooks. However, with Hoakes gone, their future looks very bleak.

R CLAIMS
OLVEMENT"

McBoddle
ent Correspondent

*McSwindle, Chair of
Council's Finance
med that the hole in
is caused by aliens.*

cil vaults on Tuesday, to
was safe. Suddenly, there
ite light. When I could
-like thing was rushing
full of notes," said the
his holiday home in the

McYurnikt said that,
IcSwindle's statement,
an arachnid from Alpha
rd and help them with

PEARE

at it takes to star in
Dramatic Society's
n of *Hamlet*?

---

er people's nose hairs?

rs protruding from other
with seeing nasal forests
e? Try the

-Tron ©

nose-hair detector.
ose comes within five
Tron© will emit a series
h bright red, and a pre-
Danger—Nose Hair" over
ver.

D

ripes. Very friendly. Collect
with secure garden.
oo big and one "just right."

e return to imon mith.

CUPCAKE
COMPETIT

Police were called ye
stop a battle between
Cupcake Society at t
It was said the one m
cheese and bacon rat
Complaints escalated
turned into a war zo
frosting and sprinkles.
whipped cream injur

NEW ROAD
SET TO DE

Campaigners have
protested Greenshore
Superhighway and the
District's most famous

"This is intolerable," said campaigner Anthony
McRanty.
The original r
estate owned
Mr Arrow-Gh

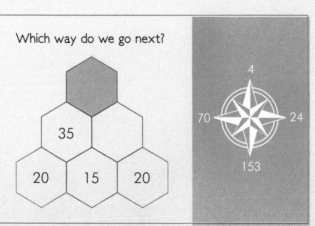

Which way do we go next?

35

20   15   20

4
70   24
153

Anatomy Alley

The Emotional Rollercoaster

APPENDIX ARCADE
Removed for safety reasons

The World of Words

Nostrilator

Digestatron

The Digestatron

I think I can see another envelope! **We need to pick the torch whose light leads to the envelope.** The letter on the correct torch will tell us which way to go next.

Can you spot Granville? He's gone wandering off again ....

The good old days! Sigh.

Henry Hoakes was born in 1898. At the age of eleven, he went to a boarding school called Bolton Towers. It was very pet-friendly, so of course I went with him.

So, thanks to Henry, I got a good education. Also, unlike every other anteater in the world, I didn't have to spend my time looking for ants. He had shipments of them sent to Bolton Towers every week from Gorblimey & Spode, the famous London delicatessen - curried ants, chocolate ants, ants-in-the-hole, ants-on-a-stick, Ant Supreme, Baked Ants Alaska, as well as good old favorites like ant'n'chips and ants-in-your-pants. Yum!

I'm getting off the point. The point being that I became the best-educated anteater in the world. It also turned out that I was good at music. Jazz music was very popular in those years, and I formed the Boltonians' Hot Jazz Quartet.

The annual pet show was the highlight of the school year, though it was not just an ordinary pet show. This was a talent contest. Henry and I won every year.

No one else came close, though one sour-faced boy tried every year to win with his snooty poodle, Prunella. The boy had no imagination and, to be honest, Prunella had no talent. Oh, she could do the usual dog tricks, but that was it. I ended up feeling a bit sorry for her, though. She clearly didn't like doing the tricks and I suspect that she didn't like the boy much, either.

Back Row: Anthony Eather   Roy Golin
nt Row: Sam O'Flage   Oliver Arrow-Ghent   Henry Hoakes

1909

1911

1913

BOLTON TOWERS

Pupil's Name......*Henry Hoakes*.................... Date..*Spring 1912*....

Subject	Comments
English	*Excellent*
History	*More than excellent*
Science	*Really, really good*
French	*Très, très, très bon. Vraime*
Geography	*Has put the school on the*

Signed...*D. Fleming McLemming, Headmaster*

Rules of the Grand Anti-Hoakes
& Anti-Anteater Association

Motto: Poodles Forever!
Membership is open to: (a) Me (b) Prunella

G.A.H.A.A.A. is dedicated to opposing
Henry Hoakes and all his evil schemes!
We hate Henry Hoakes!!
We hate his mouldy anteater too!!!
We will win!!!!
We will win even more!!!!!

OK, next we go ... um ....

32

14   19   13

63
64   65
62

Oh Henry, where do we go now? Why couldn't you just leave us a nice, clear message?

Head for the Bermuda Triangle puzzle. Which of the four dice will lead you to the envelope? Once you leave the dice, you cannot jump to a stone of the same color. And follow the lines—no diagonal crossings!

After Henry went away, he sent us the odd, unsigned postcard and other scraps that told us places he had visited. Maybe one of them contains a clue about where he was actually going ....

HOTEL NAPOLEON

Dear Concierge,
Please could my bill be ready for
the morning? I have to rejoin my ship.
With thanks

Room 45

76 RUE MADELEINE ANTSIRANANA MADAGASCAR

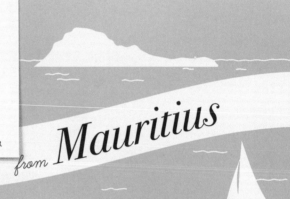

from **Mauritius**

Malta by Night

Rustbucket Line

SS Watch It! (Capt. R. Townsend)
Calling at: Malta - Rio de Janeiro -
Cape Town - Sydney - Auckland

SS Lookout! (Capt. T. Waffle)
Calling at: Marseilles - Malta -
Kenya - Madagascar - Mauritius

SS Whoopsie! (Capt. B. Cool)
Calling at: New York - San Diego - San
Francisco - Mauritius - Kenya

FLAGS OF THE WORLD
Pin Badge Collection

United Kingdom   Denmark   Greece

France   Scotland   Canada

Finland   Japan   Australia

To order, please send money by return of carrier pigeon.
We cannot be held responsible for checks lost at sea.

Le Grand Burger Bar

Double cheeseburger ....40 Fr
  avec frites (with fries)
Double, double, triple burger...63 Fr
  avec (with) tout le monde (everything)
Special veggie burger for (pah!) vegetarians.....................104 Fr
  avec le limp lettuce et le smelly cheese

143 Rue Blondin, Marseilles, France

B&O

... --- .-- .-- .-.. --.- / - ---- /
.... --- .-- .. ... .-.. / ---- --- /
... ... / .-- .-- --. --- .-.. ---
.... . / .... --- --. . / ..... --
 .- -- / .-- --. .- .-- .-.. ---
.--- . .-. .- ... . / ... . .- ---
.... . .-.. --.- / .- .-- --. .--
--- --- .-- . .-.. ---- .-- . ... ..
.- .-. . / --- .- .-- .-. --.
--- .-- . .- --- / --- .- .-.. --. .-

Do you know Morse code?
I think I saw a key on page 13.

Wild Bill's

GREAT KENYAN ELEPHANT SAFARI

Learn to shoot animals!
Bring your own camera

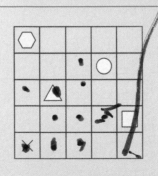

XEENENWNE

The second key! Take it, **make a note of the flag, and check the postcard for a symbol.** Then use the puzzle to tell us where we need to go next. Onward!

THE FABULOUS DANCING VENUS FLYTRAPS

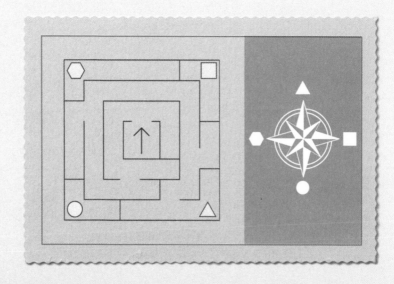

This is it! The "What to Do in an Emergency" letter! Plan Rita is going well—but **how do we read it?**

> *Pookaa Island*
> *What to Do in an Emergency*
>
> *Whatever you do, do not give way to panic.*
> *The key thing is to make sure you hold the deed to the*
> *island. Whoever has the deed owns the island.*
>
> *To find the deed you first need to get into the safe in my*
> *study. It's on the top floor of Pookaa House. No one can*
> *break into the safe—it is flame-proof, bomb-proof, and*
> *fiddle-proof. It has been tested by Biddle McTwiddle,*
> *the famous ex-safecracker, and even he gave up in*
> *despair after a week of trying to get in.*
>
> *It's too dangerous to give you the combination to the*
> *safe, in case unscrupulous people should find it.*
> *If they did, they would get the deed and all would be*
> *lost. The only way to get into the safe is to find the*
> *FOUR KEYS that I have hidden around the island.*
> *However, you have to follow the clues to find each key.*
> *When you reach the study, you will need the keys and*
> *symbols to access the safe.*
>
> *Good luck, my friends,*
>
> *The fate of the island depends on you!*
>
> *Henry*

Look out! Something just smashed through the window. It's a brick—
and there's a message attached! Things are worse than we thought ....

Listen up, fleabags!

I know you can read this! At least that too-clever-by-half, moldy old anteater can. It was me that stole Hoaksie's Grand Reveal. Wanted to have it stuffed, but it escaped and ain't been seen from that day to this. The joke is, I left a clever clue to make Hoakes think the thing had been taken back to where it came from. He took the bait, and sailed off abroad. And he ain't coming back! Ever. Hurr, hurr, hurr!

Now, to business. I've got plans for this park, but the council tells me I need the deed. I bet you know where it is. Give it to me. Now.

Why? Well, if you don't get me the deed, I will sell you all to one of the finest modern circuses—sadly forced to tour abroad since Hoakes got animal acts banned here.

I'm not unreasonable. I'm going away for a few days, giving you time to think about it. But when I come back ....

Put it this way: Get the deed for me, or start practicing your high-wire skills!

Yours ever,

A hard-hearted, double-dyed villain

NOT TOO KEEN ON ANIMALS?
LIKE TO SEE THEM DO FUNNY THINGS
THAT MAKE THEM LOOK STUPID?

THEN COME TO

GRITTY McFLITTY's

Grand Trave
fleabag sho

LAUGH! AT THE TAP-DANCING ELEPHAN
THRILL! TO HIPPOS ON A TIGHTROPE!
GASP! AT THE RHINO ON THE FLYING TRAP

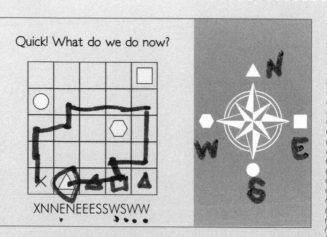

Quick! What do we do now?

XNNENEEESSWSWW

It's me again—Rita! I'm an anteater!

Some of my friends

Granville the gorilla

Elvis & Dorothy
the monkeys

Graark the seagull

Zoltan the zebra

Edward the ostrich

Tina the llama

Molly, Frank & Arthur
the bears

Abel the python

This page is where I started writing my memoirs. They will explain how I became an anteater who could answer back!

(Please don't stare at my nose like that.)

Henry & Me

My name is Rita Tamandua, and this is the story of my life. It is also the story of one of the most remarkable men who ever lived: Henry Hoakes.

Everyone's heard of theme parks where the staff dress up in costumes and pretend to be animals. Naming no names. Very amusing. Well, Hoakes Island is a place where the staff really are animals. Animals that can talk.

"That sounds crazy," I hear you say, "talking animals?" Yes, it does sound a bit bonkers, even to me at times—and I am one of them. But think about this: Have you ever really tried to have a conversation with an animal? Have a go. Banter with your budgie, chat with your cat, debate with your dog, hang out with your hamster, joke with your gerbil. The results may surprise you.

Bear in mind, however, that they might not want to talk to YOU ....

World of Words

Can you conquer the ALPHAWALL using only the vowels?

The Cliff-hanger

Punctuation Alley

Quick, let's lose them by crossing the river! Start on the stepping stone marked "Rail," and step to a stone that has a word only one letter different. Rail to Bail, and so on.

The Mighty Wordlitzer

Spine Tingler

Folded page corners!
Broken spines!
Unpaid Library fines!

Hook-a-Book

N

Sane

Sand

Laid

Land

Last

Lone

See the N, S, E and W letters on these poles. I bet it's to show us which way we need to go on the map! When we crossed the river, which pole did we get to?

I can't see the first key, though. Wait a minute, is that an envelope? I wonder what's inside?

Did I mention that I'm a genius? Well, here's the proof. Let me explain my genius idea. We need to find the "What to Do in an Emergency" letter. It's a document, a record, right? Could it be—now stay with me on this—could it be kept in the old park records office?

Quick, everyone—let's go to the old park records office!

Oh, come on, don't look so nervous. It may be dark and dusty inside, but there are no such things as ghosts or monsters, and we have a brave human with us. Let's go!

Rita Tamandua—genius

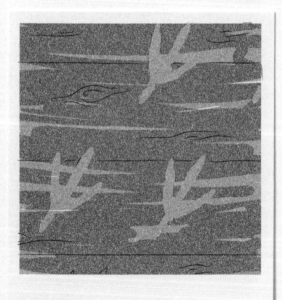

Strange tracks?

Hmm. It's a bit darker and dustier than I remembered.

What's that, Granville? You've stepped in something nasty? Well, it certainly wasn't me who left it there. Elvis? Dorothy? Anyone else? No, I thought not. We are all housebroken.

Have my hanky, Granville. No, it's all right. You keep it.

Has anyone noticed those strange tracks in the dust?

No time to investigate now—we've found the records office.

Now, we've got to search these papers carefully and systematically ....

There's a pile of boxes on that high shelf. Looks to be full of papers. Granville, could you lift them down?

Steady now, I think it's going to ....

How on earth do we find anything now?

Can you see the letter?

Quick!

No time to lose! The deed is in Henry's safe, in Henry's study, in Hoakes House, and we're still in the park office. We have to find those four keys right now!

Wait—can you hear something?

Who's that?

He doesn't look very friendly ....

Is that the villain who threw the brick?

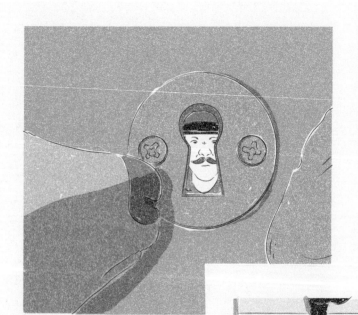

I think we should get out of here ....

He's got some evil sidekicks!

RUN!

Keep running!

Which direction do we take now?

$$\begin{array}{r} 61 \\ +51 \\ \hline 112 \end{array}$$

$$\begin{array}{r} 33 \\ +28 \\ \hline 61 \end{array}$$

(112)

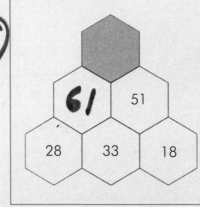

We have looked after the park ever since Henry
disappeared, all those years ago. Things like food and
other supplies were not a problem, because Henry had
arranged for them to be delivered every week, whether
he was here or not.

Maintaining the rides kept us occupied to some
extent, but there is only so much dusting, oiling and
repainting you can do before it gets really, really
BORING. The park today is as bright and clean as it
ever was, but without people it feels really quiet and
lonely. So, we got very bored. We had to try to amuse
ourselves. Some of the animals formed HOAKPADS, the
Hoakes Park Amateur Dramatic Society. They performed
all sorts of plays and shows, including a musical
version of "Robin Hood" with Granville as Robin. The
less said about that, the better ....

Otherwise, life went on its merry way. Well, not
so merry, really. We missed Henry. Even after all
this time, we hoped each day to wake up and find him
stepping ashore on the island, happy to be home with
all his friends.

I'm a Villain
by Graark

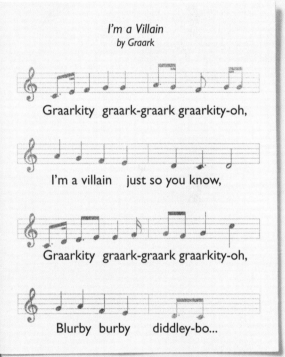

Graarkity graark-graark graarkity-oh,

I'm a villain just so you know,

Graarkity graark-graark graarkity-oh,

Blurby burby diddley-bo...

Let's keep going—where next?

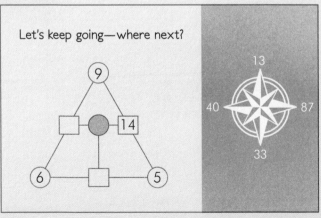

Henry's study. Well, what an amazing room. So many books and other extraordinary things. The problem is, we can't find the safe. I expect when we find it, it will also lead us to the next page. Have you got any ideas?

July 3, 1929
Journal of Henry Hoakes

It is my greatest regret that I can't save every animal in
the world. However, at least I can use my great fortune
to give some of them a good home. My plan is to build
an amusement park on Hoakes Island that will serve
as a sanctuary for my friends, but will also give them
employment and a sense of purpose.

Rita is the one to lead them—she is not only very clever,
she is also terribly good at motivating people.

Of course, there will come a day when I am no longer
here. I have made arrangements with my agents on the
mainland to keep the animals supplied with food, keep the
electricity on, etc. In this way, Granville will not have to
wonder where his next banana is coming from, nor will
Rita ever fear that she has eaten her last garlic ant.

Speaking of which, I have abandoned the idea of opening
an insect sanctuary on Hoakes Island. Rita said all of the
right things about it, but leaving an anteater in charge of
an ant farm was not wise. She was most sorry afterward,
but not half as sorry as the ants.

Henry's rescued animals were not kept as pets. All of
us became his employees and performers at the park.
Of course, as far as the public were concerned we were
just people dressed up in costumes. The idea that a
real gorilla was taking your ticket on the Emotional
Rollercoaster would just be too much for some people.
Granville is a sweet guy at heart, but doesn't take
kindly to people screaming at him.

BEANSTALK SEEDS
MIXED VARIETIES

Evil Gardening Co.
75% of Plants Guaranteed Deadly

The Greenshore Bugle
April 17, 1930

Grand Park Opening
Fart-powder millionaire Henr
today opened his new amuse
it will be something "totally o
world of entertainment. With
dressed as animals, Hoakes Is

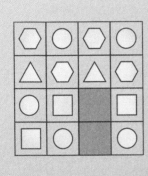

Greenshore Gazette

By Sleazy McGleazy

Entertainment Correspondent

In a move that has stunned the entertainment world, Hoakes Island has reopened! A controversial plan to demolish the park and build apartments there has been halted by Greenshore Council.

A spokesperson for Hoakes Island, who also claimed to be a genius, issued the following statement: "With the help of a hero, who wishes to remain anonymous, the long-lost deed of Hoakes Island has been rediscovered! We intend to re-open and run the island by the time Henry returns, and keep it how he wished it to be run— a place of fun for everyone."

In response to reporters' questions, Councilor Arnold Grotflick said: "Ah, well, yes. The deed. It turned up. Didn't see that one coming. Especially not delivered by a seagull. Umm, Arrow-Ghent? Who? Errr, never heard of him. And who mentioned executive apartments? Hoakes Island is the perfect place for an amusement park. Nowhere better. Always said so. Umm, can I go now?"

After being apprehended by the police on Hoakes Island, Oliver Arrow-Ghent has been convicted of trespass and threatening behavior. His sentence will be served on Hoakes Island, where he will undertake 1800 hours of community service. Dressed in a poodle costume.

Thank you, thank you, thank you!

We would never have found the deed without you! If we had failed, Hoakes Island would be in ruins by now, and all of us would be in the hands of that villain!

After this adventure, I have so much to add to my memoirs. I will send you a signed copy once they are published!

Tortoise Telegrams

"And you thought snail mail was slow!"

My dear friends! I am sure that this telegram will come as quite a shock to you. Since the SS Lookout sank I have been stranded on a remote island with only a group of grumpy penguins for company. Last week I finally managed to attract the attention of a passing ship and was rescued. The sailors happened to have a copy of the Greenshore Gazette and showed me the story about Hoakes Island. It sounds as if you have had quite an adventure. I will be home soon and look forward to hearing all about it.

Lots of love,

Henry

P.S. Did you ever find the Grand Reveal? It would be a terrible shame if we didn't retrieve it; it was the last one left in the world. Go back and check all over the island—it's very good at hiding!

The park has reopened, and, best of all, Henry has been found alive and is coming back! He's still being mysterious about the Grand Reveal, though. I wonder what it could be?

P.S. Turn to page 58

The third key! Don't forget to make a note of the flag and any symbols you find.

FONDANT FOLLY, HOAKES ISLAND

Greenland

Canada

Iceland

France

USA

Algeria

Venezuela

Brazil

Argentina

MAP OF

THE WORLD

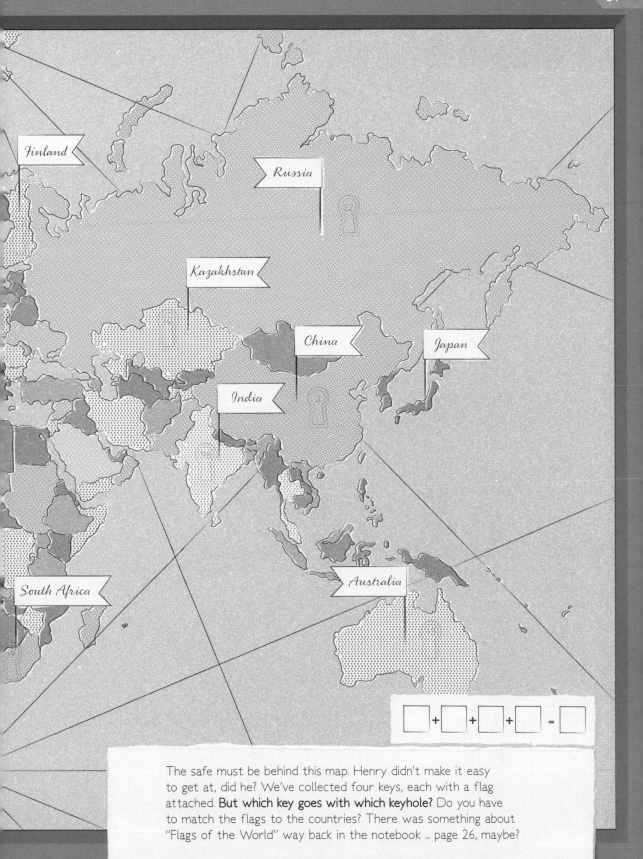

51

Finland

Russia

Kazakhstan

China

Japan

India

South Africa

Australia

☐ + ☐ + ☐ + ☐ = ☐

The safe must be behind this map. Henry didn't make it easy
to get at, did he? We've collected four keys, each with a flag
attached. **But which key goes with which keyhole?** Do you have
to match the flags to the countries? There was something about
"Flags of the World" way back in the notebook ... page 26, maybe?

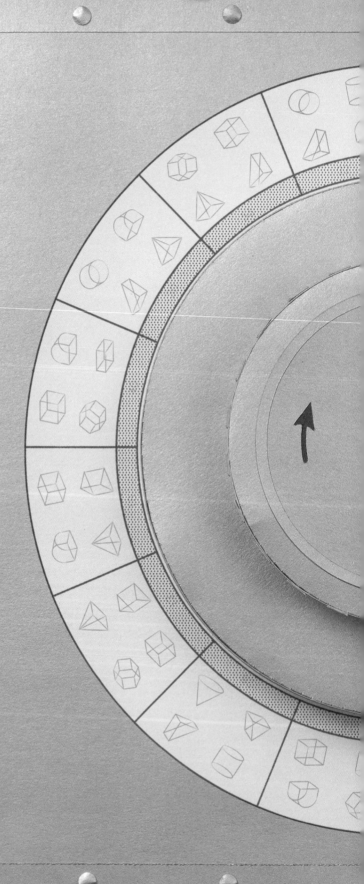

Big Red Key
Safe Co.

We've seen these symbols before!

Maybe the four symbols we found are the combination to open the safe. **Which section of the dial should we choose?** The number below it might also be a clue to the next page.

THE WATER-CYCLE FOUNTAIN

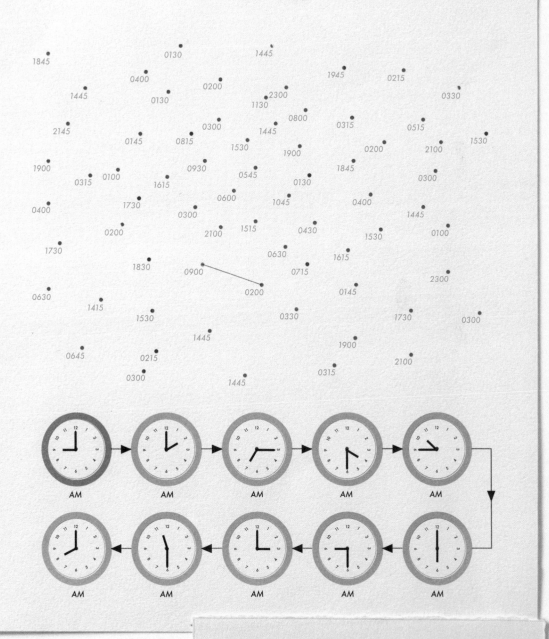

Now we have all four keys and symbols! Let's hear it for Plan Rita! This clue should take us to Hoakes House and the deed.

But which direction should we take? The numbers look like gibberish. Maybe they're linked to the clocks?

**GREENSHORE
SUBSCRIPTION
LIBRARY**

Dear Mr Hoakes,

I am pleased to tell you that the book you ordered (*The Nitwit's Guide to Hiding Important Things From Your Enemies in Places They Would Never Think to Look*) is now available to pick up from the library.

H
P
yo
ta

R

*You're almost there, you've done so well
I know you thought you'd reached the goal*

*I've one more trick that's up my sleeve
It's guaranteed to stop all thieves*

*I've put the deed inside a book
A place where avid readers look*

*Made for writing blue in color
For you it's easy to unCOVER*

*You'll need these patterns to solve the puzzle
Keep your heads—stay out of trouble*

*It's up to you, my daring friends
The place to look is at THE END*

ite my memoirs in
ook? I promise to
of it.

Rita,
The last time I lent you a book
you let the monkeys use it for
frisbee practice. The blue notebook
is very precious—use it if you
must, but take good care of it.
Henry x

Oh, Henry, you are the limit! No deed, just some notes and a cryptic
letter in back-to-front writing. Can anyone find a mirror? I'm sure
I've seen those patterns somewhere else ....

We're all together again, at last! It's so good to have Henry back after all these years. Also, we finally know what the Grand Reveal was all about. Look hard at the photo below and you might spot it ....

The Greenshore Gazette

It's NO HOAX: Hoakes Island booms as NEVER before

By Drippy McFlippy
Our Happy Endings Correspondent

As record holiday crowds board the ferries to Hoakes Island, recently rescued island founder Henry Hoakes reflects on the rebirth of his extraordinary park.

"Hoakes Island would have disappeared long since but for the faith, help, and hard work of all my friends. One of them in particular gave leadership and hope in my absence (you know who you are). And yes, I can officially confirm, you are a genius."

Answers

p.4–5
54. Go north to page 38.

p.6–7
22. Go north to page 32.

p.8–9
Hexagon. Go north to page 26.

- The flag on the key label in the envelope is the Australian flag.

- Hidden in the roof of the cottage is a square pyramid.

p.10–11
Use the floor plan on the map to work out which door leads you up to Henry's study on the third floor. The only door that gets you there is marked 42. Turn to page 42.

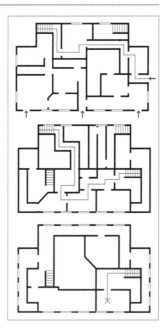

p.12–13
16. Go west to page 6.

- The Morse code reads FREE SWIMMING LESSON WITH EVERY TRIP.
- The only ferry that leaves from Greenshore is the Rustbucket Line. Henry must have taken that one.

p.14–15
55. Go south to page 40.

p.16–17
The only beanstalk that is safe to climb leads to the letter S. Go south to page 48.

- The seed packet on page 45 tells you that the only beanstalk that is not poisonous has heart-shaped leaves.

p.18–19
70. Go west to page 12.

p.20–21
Only the light from Torch E reaches the envelope. Go east to page 28.

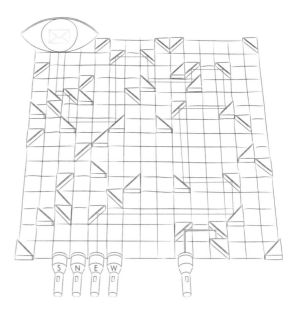

p.22–23
65. Go east to page 44.

p.24–25
The only die that takes you to the envelope at the centre has two dots. The signpost shows that two dots = west. Go west to page 54.

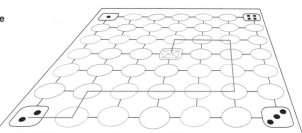

p.26–27
Circle. Go east to page 20.

XEENENWNE

- You will find the Morse code key on page 13. The message reads: SORRY TO BOTHER YOU, SS LOOKOUT HERE. HAVE HIT AN ICEBERG. PLEASE SEND HELP TO INDIAN OCEAN. CO-ORDINATES ARE GLUG GLUG GLUG.
- The only ship that visits <u>all</u> the places in the pieces of paper around the page is the SS Lookout.

p.28–29
Follow the maze to reach the triangle. Go north to page 22.

- The flag on the key label in the envelope is the Canadian flag.

- Hidden in the flowerpot of the Venus flytrap on the left is a cube.

p.30–31
Triangle. Go north to page 4.

XNNENEEESSWSWW

- Use a mirror to read the "What to Do in an Emergency" letter. It tells you that the deed is in the safe in Henry's study. You will need all four keys you collect around the island to open the safe.

p.32–33
Go west to page 36.

p.34–35
To get across the stepping stones you must step on: RAIL / BAIL / FAIL / MAIL / MAIN / MAID / LAID / LAND / SAND. The post you reach tells you to go north to page 8.

- The envelope is hidden inside a book on the "Hook-a-Book" stall.
- To reach the top of the Alphawall you climb the vowels EUAOEAEA.

p.36–37
Hexagon. Go west to page 30.

- The "What to Do in an Emergency" letter is just below and to the right of Granville.

p.38–39
112. Go east to page 34.

p.40–41
40. Go west to page 24.

p.42–43
The safe is hidden behind the map on the wall, and marked 50. Turn to page 50.

p.44–45
Go east to page 16.

p.48–49
Circle. Go east to page 14.

- The flag on the key label in the envelope is the French flag.

- Hidden in the lowest tier of the cake is a hexagonal prism.

p.54–55
Join the dots between the 24-hour clock times by the dots that correspond to the analog clocks: 0900–0200–0715–0430–1045–0600–0930–0300–1130–0800.
Once joined together, the dots form an S shape. Go south to page 10.

- The flag on the key label of the envelope is the Finnish flag.
- Hidden in the lowest tier of the fountain is a triangular prism.

p.50–51
Add up the keyhole numbers that correspond to the flags you have collected on your journey. Consult the flag pins on page 26 to work out which country each flag represents. The flags are Australia (13) / Canada (16) / France (12) / Finland (11). 13+16+12+11=52. Turn to page 52.

p.52–53
Find the group of shapes that matches the shapes hidden in the postcards you have collected. The group that matches is marked 56. Turn to page 56.

p.56–57
Use a mirror to read Henry's note. It tells you to look in the back cover of a blue notebook from his study. One that looks exactly like the one Rita has asked if she could write her memoirs in, and which you are now holding. The patterns are the key to decoding the deed. You will find this inside the back cover of the notebook.

Inside back cover
The code reads THIS IS THE DEED TO HOAKES ISLAND. WHOEVER HAS THIS DEED OWNS THE ISLAND. TURN TO PAGE FORTY SIX.

The Grand Reveal
Henry's Grand Reveal was a dodo, an animal previously thought extinct.

Did you spot...?

p.10: The dodo is hiding in the window above the front door of Hoakes House.

p.13: The note with the poodle silhouette is written by Oliver Arrow-Ghent and suggests he has taken the dodo back to Mauritius, where it came from.

p.17: The dodo is hiding in Mr. Wolf's Lupine Outfitters.

p.18: Oliver's poodle, Prunella, is in the crowd.

p.21: The dodo is having fun in the Hemoflumebin.

p.22–23: The Grand Anti-Hoakes & Anti-Anteater Association note is written by Oliver Arrow-Ghent, who also appears with Prunella, his poodle, in the background of the three photographs on page 23 and in the school photograph on page 22.

p.24: The dodo is hiding in a bush near the monkeys.

p.35: The dodo is hiding in the alphabet flowers next to the Spine Tingler.

p.36: The tracks in the dust are dodo tracks.

p.39: The dodo is hiding in a bush to the right of Edward.

p.43: There is a dodo nest hidden in the pot plant. And a poster on the wall shows mythical and extinct animals—they are all crossed out except for the dodo.

p.45: There is a partially hidden picture of a dodo under Henry's papers.

p.46: The dodo is hiding inside a balloon.

p.58–59: The dodo is hiding behind the bears on page 58. And dodo chicks are hiding in the plant on page 59.

Lost the map?
Don't panic! Just go online to www.laurenceking.com and search for "Hoakes Island" to access another copy.

Acknowledgments

Other anteaters often write to me, asking, "Rita, did you write Hoakes Island all by yourself?" Well, though I am a genius, I can't take all the credit. This book would not have happened without the help of a number of important humans. So, I would like to say a big "thank you" to these non-ant-eating people.

To begin with, Elsa, Lukas, and Luke did the reader-testing for the younger human community. Thanks a million, guys, you will always be in my heart. Are you sure that you don't want those chocolate ants we talked about?

Lynne, Simon, Daisy, and Dimitris very kindly looked at *Hoakes Island* from the grown-up point-of-view. Jasper Fry took all the lovely photographs. Finally, the book could not have been realized without the help, hard work, and enthusiastic support of Elizabeth, Chloë, Melissa, Davina, and all their colleagues at Laurence King Publishing.

Oh, I do go on a bit, don't I? The price of genius ....